T0083432

# domina Un/blued

## The Dorset Prize

*Ice, Mouth, Song* by Rachel Contreni Flynn
Selected by Stephen Dunn

*Red Summer* by Amaud Jamaul Johnson
Selected by Ray Gonzalez

*Dancing in Odessa* by Ilya Kaminsky
Selected by Eleanor Wilner

*Dismal Rock* by Davis McCombs
Selected by Linda Gregerson

*Biogeography* by Sandra Meek
Selected by the Tupelo Press Editors

*Archicembalo* by G. C. Waldrep
Selected by C. D. Wright

*Severance Songs* by Joshua Corey
Selected by Ilya Kaminsky

*After Urgency* by Rusty Morrison
Selected by Jane Hirshfield

*domina Un/blued* by Ruth Ellen Kocher
Selected by Lynn Emanuel

RUTH ELLEN KOCHER

# domina Un/blued

poems

TUPELO PRESS    North Adams, Massachusetts

*domina Un/blued*

Copyright 2013 Ruth Ellen Kocher. All rights reserved.

Library of Congress Cataloging-in-Publication Data available upon request.

ISBN 978-1-936797-19-6

Cover and text designed by Ann Aspell.

First edition: April 2013.

Other than brief excerpts for reviews and commentaries, no part of this book may be reproduced by any means without permission of the publisher. Please address requests for reprint permission or for course-adoption discounts to:

Tupelo Press
P.O. Box 1767
243 Union Street, Eclipse Mill, Loft 305
North Adams, Massachusetts 01247
Telephone: (413) 664–9611 / Fax: (413) 664–9711
editor@tupelopress.org / www.tupelopress.org

Tupelo Press is an award-winning independent literary press that publishes fine fiction, nonfiction, and poetry in books that are a joy to hold as well as read. Tupelo Press is a registered 501(c)3 nonprofit organization, and we rely on public support to carry out our mission of publishing extraordinary work that may be outside the realm of large commercial publishers. Financial donations are welcome and are tax deductible.

*To my Mother, for her faith in everyone.*

*To Paul, for his faith in me.*

# CONTENTS

# domina Un/blued

## Stealing a Woman in Broad Daylight

Near the *teatro di Marcello* noon on a very hot June day
A man on a vespa attempted to steal me. *Ciao     Bella*

So obvious. Hello hello. You speak Italian? Yes
You do.   Oh     a little.   Near the *teatro di Marcello* near

An old church also  Roman columns exposed at its sides.
*E molto caldo* I say clearly. He nods. Very hot it is.

*E molto caldo.*

# D/domina: Issues Involving Translation

---

Possessive case for the word 'slave' does not exist in Italian.

The slave  owned  not own  nor owns

Nor evolves. Nor provision  any  make consonant belonging.

---

EXERCISE 17.


On the streets of America today a little tear-gas powders the up

Air     buildings behind the blue clouds gleam   not a century old

un-ruined

Forum become column become a basket from beneath acanthus

climbs

Toward the heavy stone tablet   the funereal items arranged inside covered

The woven movement    her sisters fingers          her daughter's hewn

Grass taken late      the day's wet mist     Tiber returned arterial

Flow   heat   stock     dry enough to bundle

Without mold.


Long ago   everyone knew what mist destroyed.

On the streets of America today shields

pushed against rocks. The air gusts of what after blue

gray becomes    what gray always has hoped    has

sought low crouching at the foot        weapons

clicking the clack boots march which neither good nor bad is

both      but everything.

*la tratta degli schiavi del blocco note*

the writing done by the slave in a notebook

*la scrittura di fatto la tratta degli schiavi del blocco note*

the writing a black slave does in the notebook of her grandfather.

*la scrittura di un nero schiavo non nel blocco note di suo nonno.*

the writing of a black slave whose grandfather was also a slave but
not black

*la scrittura di un nero schiavo cui nonno e stato anche uno schiavo  ma non nero*
black is only a thing the slave owns that is nothing
*il nero è solo una cosa che il proprietario di schiavi che non è nulla*

repeat after me
*ripetere        dopo                                    di*

         *me*

the writing done by the slave in a notebook belongs to no one
no one belongs to the slave

| Translation Exercise | Esercizio di traduzione |
|---|---|
| the ferns grow in heat | *le felci crescono in calore* |
| the ferns grow in heat | *le felci crescono in calore* |
| the acanthus grow like the ferns | *l'acanto crescono come le felci* |
| it is very hot | *fa molto caldo* |
| it is hot | *è caldo* |
| warm | *caldo* |
| blazing | *sfolgorante* |
| the handcuffs begin with me | *le manette iniziano con me* |
| i am the lock and the key | *io sono la serratura e la chiave* |
| i am the key and the slave | *io sono la chiave e lo schiavo* |
| i am the slave and the key | *io sono lo schiavo e la chiave* |
| the keys | *i tasti* |
| i belong to | *io appartengo a* |
| my self not my sex | *me stesso, non il mio sesso* |
| i do not belong here | *io non appartengo a questo posto* |
| the columns are capped in acanthus | *le colonne sono chiuso nel acanto* |

| | |
|---|---|
| and a death tablet | *e una morte tavoletta* |
| you can always talk about | *si può sempre parlare di* |
| architecture | *architettura* |
| i belong to him | *io appartengo a lui* |
| endurance | *resistenza* |
| i am not afraid of you | *io non io paura di te* |
| i have lied | *io mentito* |
| i belong to no one | *io appartengo a nessuno* |
| still | *ancora* |
| i am not afraid of you | *io non io paura di te* |
| in Ghana | *in Ghana* |
| i am not afraid of you | *io non io paura di te* |
| in Venice | *a Venezia* |
| the columns are capped in acanthus | *le colonne sono chiuso nel acanto* |
| because the lost meaning | *perché il senso perduto* |
| of classical architecture | *dell'architettura classica* |

| | |
|---|---|
| says the journal of decadent | *dice il giornale della decadente* |
| aesthetics is speculation | *l'estetica è la speculazione* |
| i have lied | *io mentito* |
| endurance in Ghana is endurance | *resistenza in Ghana è la resistenza* |
| in Venice. | *a Venezia.* |
| still | *ancora* |
| the key and the slave | *la chiave e lo schiavo* |
| are very tricky | *sono molto difficili* |
| nearly interchangeable for the student | *quasi intercambiabili per lo studente* |
| of a language which depends | *di un linguaggio che dipende* |
| so much | *tanto* |
| on difference | *sulla differenza* |
| the acanthus grow like the ferns | *l'acanto crescono come le felci* |
| it is very hot | *fa molto caldo* |
| it is hot | *è caldo* |
| warm | *caldo* |
| blazing | *sfolgorante* |

| | |
|---|---|
| the handcuffs begin with me | le manette iniziano con me |
| i am the lock and the key | io sono la serratura e la chiave |
| i am the key and the slave | io sono la chiave e lo schiavo |
| i am the slave and the key | io sono lo schiavo e la chiave |
| the keys | i tasti |
| i belong to myself | io appartengo a me stesso |
| my self not my sex | me stesso, non il mio sesso |
| i do not belong here | io non appartengo a questo posto |
| the columns are capped in acanthus | le colonne sono chiuso nel acanto |
| and a death tablet | e una morte tavoletta |
| you can always talk about | si può sempre parlare di |
| architecture | architettura |
| i belong here | io appartengo a questo posto |
| i do not belong to you | io non ti appartengono |
| the columns are capped in acanthus | le colonne sono chiuso nel acanto |
| because someone placed a basket | perché qualcuno ha messo un cesto |
| on the grave of a slave girl | sulla tomba di una schiava |

## D/domina: Daughter

I cannot help but imagine your death if—then
a brief underside of porous leaf slick in its place


as you catch your last breath    know how it costs to lose
the smallest thread of universe


so what you feel becomes
not the sky opening in front of you


wall of gray on gray    gray that matters
in its far away hitch to land


and within that conversion
your loss as a first nothingness


a failing you peel back to find
the way you held your fork

—

quiet rocking    earth's movement
saturated in spheres of mayhem    constant

refusal of stillness. Dirt moves under you    the leaf
moves and is relieved    cold moves

knowing it will fail. As you turn over
to departure    grow into what has left

suit your return    not as memory but
beginning pulled out of bed

acid for the charmed endings we make
cosmos-orange particles glimpsed around stars

solid in our want of them    opaque beyond
the dispersal they are    being draped galaxy.

## D/domina Speaks of [the Search for] G/god(s)


when the Messengers/angels are speechless … when the
Messengers/angels

stop sweeping their porches and look to the western sky which
undoes itself

for lack of tacking down—drifts away unmoored    a sailboat that
has oars

bent at the angle elbows are bent when you read a book or

hold the face of a love who kneels before you    looking up    the
light or

mercy passing through the lens of his left eye so that it floats there
flickers
when

the Messengers/angels don't know what to say as  sycamores declare
their
sovereignty


—

as the tides hesitate their return    as the engines

that populate all of the Americas sputter and stop … and your
lover's eye
just

floats there    a continent unto itself drawing every spark and flash of
flint
into it

so the explosion you witness is not your own heart sending out red
flares

but the eye    the lens of the eye deflecting a confetti of lenses each
your

lover's eye again catching light—and with all this light still the
Messengers/

angels come to their porches and stare at the disappearing sky as though the human heart—even the burning shards exploding

skyward—


has outlived its myth—

## D/domina: G/gnosis


That summer the body forgot hesitation
Wandered mountains    met boys

Whose faces lost soft curves    spirit edged
stubble       She called it

tried to become one with it again but    The body
floated afternoons in birch creek pools    cutoffs

soaked through    legs learning skin and skin.
Mornings    feet caked black with culm

The body took paths through waste-land woods
followed her back to the apartment    Her body

hid from its parents    Forgot its sisters    Bathed
each morning as though performing ritual

leaving    Her body knew before she knew
Soon    like hesitation    It would forget return.

## D/domina's Feet


Three couplets of an epic are nothing to sneeze at    The grocer

Says not to *i pomidori* but to *la donna. Signora*—


                These woods equal all woods. Any construct works

to

[equal].


                These woods are all woods. These woods [colon]

all

Woods.


*Signora* leaves her body *perché* perched in front of *la*

*frutta verdura carrello* and in spirit mindlessly walks


                These woods [period] All Woods [period] No

matter

How hard 'All

                Woods' desires to be only wood    all woods is all

woods.

All ways

into the Forum     other ghosts suspicious [period] The arbor vita
twists around

Her feet. The grocer has seen this happen before and turns to the
oranges
                    The woods love you better when you call your
name them.
                    The stream could care less caught in its own wet
whisper.

## The Law of Suspects

failure is not silent. with it the trees creak. leaves rattle

hear? *da dee dum dum dum da dee dum dum*
*o-o-o Oligar-r-r-rchy* of crow loon dove feathered hats.

*shhhhhhhh.* the sound of a whisper is the sound of something
which begs to be said. imagine every cut coming back to you

paper cut. guillotine. olives. almonds. vermouth
trees in the mountains there writhe through each breeze

an empire begins this way    rowed orchards with heavy fruit

plenty-stained peaches. *Marie Marie* … enforcement [is] justice
no      vermouth is not cut but cuts    this is true. almonds resist

the blade    roll away    yes. but somewhere within them is perfect
sliver. one century forgets another always within a pitched vibration.

bus engines revving fail too. chimed retreat. spin sounds our ears.

## Translation Exercise II

*31-year-old Black man in Lombardy  Italy*
*Looking For:*


My desire


How are they? I do not know! I can speak only for myself heard

that is  I

can tell as I see others


Some people I sweet  delicate  who would aggressively

*animaleschi* who would elegant  refined  who would sport it seems to me

me

that *oguno*

exactly as you wish


I like to go to the bottom of things        innovation and novelty

attract.

I like space    living sometimes totally opposed to.


I assure you that I like the game and fun  the transgression  me

*irresistibilmente*

provided no sections codified  approved

stereotyped

I do not think that I am boring

One that resembles more to normal

not so studied.


If I propose to transgress so original and spontaneous

I hardly shot back.

## Ouidah

It could be that he looked like Caliban.
His flicked tongue intrigued us.


We understood when we saw him:
within us is a spiral that can make
a rock    a tree


And then    besides that small fractal
where we anchored    hitched our lives to a body
our bodies to land


the sea emptied us. Accepted us
in rasp and shudder.


Their bones cannot help
but railroad ships across the sea.
Think of angular and ugly

the ocean floor spiked deep.


If there were flames underwater

they would be black shaped

running bodies

become wave.

## D/domina: Feast


Some things cannot be wrapped.

                        I answer as always

it began with Caravaggio red and someone

nods to my left

        nothing further behind the nodding

        the tall white corner gray-halved losing light



        Empire flavors bread or parches crust

crisp or seeps from duck plated endive or spreads

thin the brie spreads the drapes spreads the scarf

Spreads across the naked male lap

pastoral all among this else As also



the table cloth resistant white

edged against each other simplicity arranged on top.

        Butter-sex. Onion-sex. Spoon.

        Napkins not unlike the table thread white

        thread woven thread skein thread loom At times

        shroud especially in retrospect as the ghost called up

        mutes

a tall cowered corner As legs adjust beneath

An ankle crossed in uncrossed Her hands

                panic in her lap All hands in all

the laps wonder if should they panic


will bread pudding save them Pinot poached

pears Rosemary apple tart last    a short pause


Indeed we have come after a great disaster

## Domina


What boy in leather pants

to gaze but    O    the long hallway that wields you finally


wild breasted thing.


Imagine he cries    He stiffens    The carcass of a derailed train that

sits

at an angle to its track


so together you make an arrow pointing away.


Imagine he walks into the club & the purple lasers him into two so

one eye

belongs to the him coming toward you and one

stays just a step behind    measures the pace    stalks the beat

       him coming


towards you    his reflection pooled across every mirrored wall

Mercury's quick desire but    O    only him wantless to look at others


as they look at him but    O    if he could see—and to see to see

to see them see him see


*Sweet brute*


*drop*


*to your knees.*

## D/domina: Empire


First by desert    warm seas    rapid diversification

rise

almost all a county in the North

the passage of a population

ceremonial county bounded west

the Sea the south

the southeast by the east lies directly to the north.


*One beautiful Kingdom*


Generations of mountain

the highest point all territory over above the sea

parts found northernmost    the county in and around.


The most popular: Christianity    Buddhism    Islam:

race age income mobility attainment ownership status

as well as    over time … over time.


The human change. There is no absolute

whereas the fields should not be used interchangeably with

a collection of beings.

Such may be anything

which relates to wants able to appeal to

this people    art    literature (in which they are ) theatre    music:

any medium affected by forms    appeals.


*The meaning of a branch is an absolute value*


Any human view:    an object or lack thereof    regardless of its

purpose.

A cup may be ornament. A painting deemed any skill. Mastery.


The intention of nature means Tolstoy    a use indirect

one person to another; the work    therefore    the mind    the

creator

the mimesis or deep roots in the philosophy of …

## A Romance

Someone will die before it's over.

In the beginning   even the cats roaming *un teatro di torri* would have
an opinion: The matter of all seduction bleats most at tides and the
hindrance of gravity

interfering orbits of refuge not garbage but useful-unused-man-made
things

potions claim some also the eye's opium O of erection the want gaze
Kasha Silverman calls *not* a look   *not* the same dilated seeing.

Taste that? Curdled syrup too hot in cream. Bee sting. Sun-seared
shoulders metallic salty (kiss?)—Love has stayed too long   disrobed
too soon   cum before the wine has breathed

Leans … Hears whisper teeth rake breath from lip the neck bent
open   assuming … Listen … pause …

*Tell me what to do*

## D/domina: ~~Ode to~~ Violence

At the kitchen table your place remains set

The cupboard waits with open doors After we

walk under the threat of rain    sew the dank

hours together    fill the space you've left

our cheeks without sting    our cheeks

our cheeks    our fists    we watch you tempered

broadcast on New York City streets    The cop

an actress whose makeup    makes her look

un-made-up    Her partner

Her partner in love with her

Bring us back to you    red streak boredom

expectation unfolded    smacked down need




How you make us wait your entrance    watch for

your cue    How you make us want

## D/domina

sorry to request

sorry to Y/you to be unworthy

(this morning on the train Y/you show M/me that Y/you are)

(this morning on the train Y/you yolk as uniform as the egg's shell)

(an old man looks at me and H/he has Y/your bitter)

G/goddess

i thank Y/you again

(the egg knows an order)

i request not demand Y/you please

please Y/you for Y/you to serve as serving pleases Y/you


Y/you must help Y/you must show Y/you must

if it pleases Y/you to me then it will be so if Y/you must


W/we have our purpose as singular as one sided

(the egg is thick and useful) (the egg is discipline as Y/you are)


Y/you see Y/you must to me beneath to Y/yours

i am sorry for saying "Y/you must"

retract humbly that request to Y/you

beneath Y/your to me for Y/you unworthy




i am not

## D/domina: Statue of a Man Eating His Heart Out

Plaster studies body in this form. Lesson

sculpted—how else to make shape

know the urge to fail    as skin fails

crouch    as shoulders crouch    turn at the ankle

less a postured defeat than a body

interrupted release of tremor    pull.

She sees him        folded body

worked out of her hands

thinks

Even the inanimate                should

                                not bare this.

## D/domina Paints

Far away  your canvas not blank but not there:

beige largeness closer but more and more movement.

You paint green slate black blue sand neutral—not *his* Sounds in the

Grass

not *his* Composition   really   but memory

or the imaginings of you as who you become as though the ahead

could be witness to this demise of your own

going forward

un-stricken. The installation of a world's collapse

pebbled as if the painted sand evolved into boulder or the boulder's

regression became collected   pure.   The barn's cold air

would catch your breath in frost as you watched him paint. Absorb

him. But how to disappear completely   then   the dark lines or

not lines   here   again




from far away the canvas is not blank but also not yours—

also a shadow   perhaps of you standing in front of it   sun

behind you   phone ringing through one white room

to the next   him   never and always there

## D/domina: Pastoral


Can the Tree        Again

anchor the center of a gallery floor

*sfumato* leaves acrylic in their tint

canvas      already      or verse

bark even oak

stand simply rooted to green

Another city lawn—

Force the Tree into Pastoral

Sonnet


Then dull and dull days. Few

moments      Fewer to steal

adjectives abate      Fired kiln

Syntax


How much can an acorn become

Sadly capped

above its oval bulbing

its nippled tip

brown fighting ochre to cover it?


1917 Society of Independent Artists Exhibit:

Duchamp submits a urinal The universal center

the post I/importance lens of his life

He called it "Fountain"


Imagine the poor porcelain form

a cupped white hand

       The center of the room

glints back harsh light


an opaque theory    An expansion

       The ordinary

needing more than:


urinal   you think   Urinal

and then   Tree

## D/domina: Hybrids : G/gods

The way the onion spindles itself out of earth equals emotion rather

than

reason                        in two respects,


First    sky translated—a particular sequence thus implied:


                    cloud    moon    star
                    Second    in part


light succeeding shadow—


unwarranted possession

            the two entwined.

            Mutual derogation. The onion    itself

sweet or bitter. Both.

                    Life within the form

scripted in consequence.



Lovely weed    flowering body



indifferent to the anatomy of taste as

              property                          décor.

# D/domina: Mule

*As the beautiful thing confers on the perceiver the gift of life*
*so the perceiver confers on the beautiful thing the gift of life*

— ELAINE SCARRY

His cock spins    that not possible

opposite of universe    starry


spiral unfolded    beheaded

pearled ass clench    useless swell


(a wolf in his chest    ears back

fur bristled black    white then gray)


nostrils tendril inward    hollow the face

the skull's caverns

the straddled sternum's cleft paddle

ribs reach     cage


his mute heart          reverberate

the internal walls indifferent


dumb pump         hooves

each in love with the ground's small


eruption           dust billowed at the gallop's

clap clip  slowly raised foot coming


back again always to earth's bridge

straw's give   stone's round resistance.

## D/domina: Matter


The cat lands on the front walk of his home

          perhaps in the middle of the night

mouse escaping narrowly



          skid and tires maybe

          or kids drunk with the smell of June

bass in two-four time running through



          soft tissue they call love

          but no matter

here is a dead animal

Whose life has spiraled vertically upward

        past the tip of the sycamore's highest leaf

hovers just there beyond the body's reach




so the boy pushed by his father to get off the couch

        pulls on thick gloves for a larger man

        picks up the shovel      stares




down




        split muff specked gray

        tawny in the low afternoon here      St. Louis

            I drive to work        wonder about my body

when it will     how much I should

and his eyes


            find mine passing in the too old Honda for

someone

with so much school     I see

            his face wrenched

The disgust we meet death with


            as though it will retreat        unwelcome

            I think

            his eyes and mine


—

50

find one path

        a windshield     speed between us

I want to slow down    look longer




see him   how young he is

how beautifully removed

## Becoming D/domina

Don't smile too much. Make sure
you're smiling enough.

Nod when people speak. Seem interested
while they're speaking. Don't get personal.

Watch the progress of the neighbor's lawn.
Be bothered by dandelion and clover.

Name your daughter something your parents

would not have chosen. Expect them


to love the name. Argue if they don't.

Reminisce about the struggles of childhood


the bike you didn't have    your absent father

your mother drinking Scotch over Rice-a-Roni


forgotten brownies for your sleepover.

Curse cicadas as they tremor July's evening

with a 17-year-old song. Wax the car yourself

and dread sudden rain. Talk about being thin. Vote

for someone. Drive everywhere.

Join a gym. Imagine no

girl dragging her leg behind her

through a street in Karbala.

Don't ask questions. Shop.
Do not seem racist. Fit. Think about an affair.




Don't talk about the news. Hold your breath
when you pray. Remember




yourself through the eyes of the last person
who saw you. Go to the fireworks.




Don't ask where Karbala is. Accept the cicadas. Sit
on your porch.    Wonder at the dullness of summer.

## D/domina: G/gnosis II


Evening blindfolds you          Quickly

Without asking          *Are you comfortable*




black mask deprivation          Awards each other sense

great hold          The grass musk strong          The pasture

two miles away




Your throat's coat          Hay-tongue soot-lung freeway-filled

Ears engines          wind          meeting

Why            You wonder just now

How the mind reaches     Out from          Gray case muteness




Makes a world

Itself the image      So finally you sit centered-      -all.




Dark corners want

Drawn to the whale call      your spleen      shriek caw

        heart you know as pounding

The *please please please* bound hands hold.

Cold tile under your bare feet         does not belie chill earth.

The mirror envies such       Inner dimension.



Pallid stars    found not yet    you

blind still    goose-fleshed

without      what it means      to see.

# Un/blued

the columns are
  capped with
    acanthus
empire Empire
E/empire
empire Empire
E/empire
empire Empire
E/empire
empire Empire
E/empire
empire Empire
E/empire
empire Empire
E/empire
empire Empire
E/empire
empire Empire
E/empire
empire Empire
E/empire
empire Empire
E/empire
empire Empire
E/empire

empire Empire
E/empire
baby, baby, o
baby
girl

the columns are
  capped with
    acanthus
empire Empire
E/empire
empire Empire
E/empire
empire Empire
E/empire
empire Empire
E/empire
empire Empire
E/empire
empire Empire
E/empire
empire Empire
E/empire
empire Empire
E/empire
empire Empire
E/empire
empire Empire
E/empire
empire Empire
E/empire
empire Empire
E/empire

empire Empire
E/empire
baby, baby, o
baby
girl

the columns are
  capped with
    acanthus
empire Empire
E/empire
empire Empire
E/empire
empire Empire
E/empire
empire Empire
E/empire
empire Empire
E/empire
empire Empire
E/empire
empire Empire
E/empire
empire Empire
E/empire
empire Empire
E/empire
empire Empire
E/empire
empire Empire
E/empire
empire Empire
E/empire

empire Empire
E/empire
baby, baby, o
baby
girl

## D/domina: Look


sun yellow

the bottle falls out of the bottom paper bag soaked through smashed

40

grass nearby cut and clumped. grass clippings. grass smell. grass

green and gasoline. engine. night

streetlights come on




say    night come on. the flap is not pigskin. is not rubber. is not wax

but bleeding and human  is not a hand waving down cars.

streetlights come on

not white light yet against exhaust not yet black sheltered mountains.

every puddle reflects     fender reflects     steeled glass windows of

each home


reflects now white light not yet. the evening kneels before you

bowed

reticent. what does her face look like looking away from you

unsure whether to rise or stay. bowed. this morning you would have

eaten every

last bit of your meal had the night come to you like this      then
had she gotten on her knees      bowed before you      opened the
split frame of your flesh like the bulleted


window    the twisted shrapnel unwrapping the calm. the evening
lifts her chin    stares past you as though    already you leave. spiral
not back to her. not


gaze shiny street    not bleed. not bleed. a family of locust will
remember

—

your breath     the lull terminating for you the drum beats     one
love   sway of dreadlocks that year. the car passes away     and you
with evening     here

## Transatlantic Catalogue with Distant Voice Refrain

dominico brings the fig tree from calabria    neighbors laugh
*fratello* joseph pines the wife lost to his brother   large hands
slapping flour her cast vowels widening the echo of the hall

I.
those names and chest sit high up their stupid
girl broke-hearted over suede shoes and those

cheekbones stupid girl white blues

dominico brings the fig all the way from …
he ignores pennsylvania cool nights (chill fall wraps it)
builds a fire to warm fruit from home deep dreamed

II.

girl's man plays piano plays women plays

soul's bringing then bringing them


bass shadow paris lampposts swooning.

dominico brings a tree with him     neighbors laugh

his daughter bites the fruit's dark skin round bruise

filled with sugar.


his daughter tastes Motown white blues broke

-hearted piano that broke-hearted

broke-hearted girl.

## Near *Torre Argentina*

The cars near *Torre Argentina* seem to understand how

unimportant Caesar has become against the failing

sky of this century's Rome. Against the failing sky

here in Rome the women walk quickly and do not

look back to a doorway which creaks

*ciao bella* as one passes by. As one passes by

the fountain wishes to freeze in mid-

arc in order to hear the soft pad of her sandals.

In mid-arc she sees the water's wish disperse as

falling droplets into a pool and imagines all the doors

in this city closing at once    the traffic paused in the midst

of whir    the jets above baying as lambs bay. The cats

watch her pass    seem to understand    also    how

unimportant this woman    her dress a cardinal flare of red

her feet    also    determined

## D/domina: Forgetting the Tree

When you live in a city

cow pastures marked by the divots

of hooved lumbering forward

remain as much a myth as constellations

supposedly sleeping between stars.

Dung heaps keep worries to themselves.

Grass hushes wind to its hubris.

Clouds roll over fields sleepy

as a girl out of bed too soon as soil

retreats to the earth's imagination.

The planet silent except for cut rock

mountain backs heaved up—

only in the green light flash of traffic

sent forward

lurch of movement

never really still

underneath sirens the clip

clapping of people

moving from this place to that

only in the small

squared parcel of gray atmosphere

veiling the crown of your city's height

beyond the tipped steel tits

can you remember that I was

not always rooted to this avenue

nor caught in the pull of the sky drowned out

by parking lot lights    speck-less

G/gods' storyboard    stars.

## Anno Domini

A far point rendezvous. A smoke plume.

[a fire. fog standing from the valley. an eruption meets salt water. the factory walls burn out. war-close. the core melts. the engine flames. a cloud. the bomb detonates. mist goes askew. split dew mounts the river bank.]

*I love you*

A smoke plume   a jet; vapor.

A Taxi hum down The long Ethiopian neck

The driver pitches into the left turn.

*The anniversary of my crime:*

*Leaving Atlanta: East: Jesus Saves*

Car 4–7–1–2. no food. no drink

dangerous essential Slick    serrated lists:

bristle    ginger    peel    smoke

Lithium tarnished-copper: Penny on heads:


*Hop  skip  jump  girl  jump  skip  hop:*

*The first gods    the next gods    the last gods:*

*The angels    of which    there are none.*


Leaving here today. frayed seat belt

Now ornamented departure     sweet Backwards pace

                        Blueberry scone. coffee brewing …


*leave leave leave*

*Until you come back    we will not Say your name.*


Every city [is] every city. Every city [is] every shore.

[great love serves predictably    a cyclic story]

—

A cliff bound to disintegrate    bound again


Lava tongue    bound back plates

Risen

                    *little deaths  little deaths  little deaths*


risen ... bound again: cliff  cliff  cliff—

## D/domina: Lotus


The traveler stayed

lost: child gone

spouse—a warm pace


away     the construction of each

Neighborhood     an effigy of bird calls

ruinous against a could-be


silence

so seductive you will kill

the breath of intrusion

easily as memory

splayed. Why look up? Why notice

sky static and crippled with

movement

of weather that forms despite you


or noon's bulbous seconds


rolling off as so many drips into

a clear bladder

that takes any shape it holds—under the first

skin of earth is a compass    is a satchel

is a kite with bow-tie ribbons

is a ferret skull

is a sandwich with brown mustard

but mostly distraction

comes solicited. Warranted. Do not ask for return.

Do not ask for what easily finds you.

## M/mediation I Dominance


The once has never said

Nor the next day stammered

To you the black bird calls across pine

To you the creek is in a rush

Pity first sky spread so thin

Pity next the water bottle crushed at the road's edge

Discard can never diminish its grip on

What cannot stop that which

Drink the reservoir in an untapped gulp

Breathe carbon breath freeways

Forget that within you a knife

Forget the red storm of wanting to

## M/mediation II Submission


he says … the sky is beautiful …

you say … yes the cloud is lined.

he says … no, really …

you say … yes, it is so.

everything now defeated

couched against the forever loveliness

of ever after. but how unseemly

how cliché. how awful the art of real and pathetic

happiness. a poem about happiness

cannot succeed. a poem about happiness

makes you search your gut

for the last borne pang

## D/domina: Parable: Become

The problem with the myth:
you love the monster's glass stare.

You cheer her oval pupil     yellow eye.
Men's bones snap between her molars.

She roams woods spitting out
shards of boys     so many

even the lame felled at the feet of our
indifference     that sorrow.

Feel her desire jackhammer
through you     the hunch     the long claw

the drooling need in this creature.

## D/domina: Issues Involving Interpretation

---

EXERCISE 44.

The word has no life of its own          despite what the writer
tells you.
Behind the sword is no quivering hand worn into life's hilt    no arm
swaying the wind in dying movement.
There is only the word       sword.

Outside trees live without language and tip toward whatever sun

manages through a thinning atmosphere of dust

ice    vapor.


The life of each branch balances on what the tree affords it. The soil

holds the tree without language or pity.


But there is no tree in this poem    only the word    tree. There is

no speaker who

entreats you to imagine

the tree standing solitary in a green field   specked with clover

rising in tufts of almost transparent cream.


There is no field. There is no clover    no green. You listen

anyway. Hear a voice follow you into the afternoon    Language

crosses a clearing    the stark way a thing    revealed

when thinned clouds expose better light.

You    the tree    tip toward words as they bring outward

inner form.

## ACKNOWLEDGMENTS

I would like to thank Toi Derricotte and Cornelius Eady for their support; my Cave Canem family, especially Caroline Micklem, Sarah Micklem, Alison Meyers, Terrance Hayes, Jacqueline Jones LaMon, Tyehimba Jess, Amanda Johnson, and Camille Rankine, for their work at retreats where some of these poems were written or rewritten; Yusef Komunyakaa, Nikky Finney, Al Young, Colleen McElroy, Ed Roberson, Claudia Rankine, Marilyn Nelson, for their writing mentorship; Kathy Fagan, Lynn Emanuel, Jim Schley, Jeffrey Levine, Douglas Kearney, Ross Gay, and Matthew Shenoda for closely reading the many excerpts and incarnations of this project; Jake Adam York for his generous offer; Latasha Natasha Nevada Diggs, Adrien Matejka, Duriel Harris, Krista Franklin, Mary Gannon, Wendy S. Walters, and Paul Smith for spiriting me through; the Cave Canem Foundation, Yaddo, and the Department of English at the University of Colorado for financial support and sponsorship; and Jacqueline Scott for ushering me through the streets of Rome, Venice, and Lido as I searched for the heart of this book.

*domina Un/blued* is an experiment in palimpsestic writing. The present text has been built upon the ruins of two previous manuscripts, *Hybrids & Monsters* and *The Slave's Notebook,* now buried and visible only in glimpses when unearthed. For that reason, many poems that make up the foundation of this book cannot be found here. I thank the following publications in which poems, versions of poems, and now effaced poems from previous facades of the manuscript appeared:

*Callaloo:* "D/domina: Issues Involving Interpretation" (as "Issues Involving Interpretation") and "Gabriel Slicing Onions"; *Cartier Review:* "Stealing a Woman in Broad Daylight," "Transatlantic Catalogue with Distant Voice Refrain," and "Translation Exercise II"; *Denver Quarterly:* "D/domina: Daughter" (as "Daughter"); *Ditch:* "Doctrine of Release" and "D/domina: Mule" (as "Anatomy of a Mule"); *Drunken Boat:* "Continuum" and "Learning to Be Middle Class Checklist"; *Eleven Eleven:* "M/mediation I Dominance" (as "M/meditation I Dominance") and "M/mediation II Submission" (as "M/meditation II Submission"); *Superstition Review:* "Domina: Forgetting" (as "Lesson: Daphne as Tree Forgetting"), "Domina: Issues Involving Translation" (as "The Slave's Notebook"), "Domina: Looking" (as "Lesson: Looking Away"), and "Domina: Lotus" (as "Lesson: She as a Lotus Eater"); and *Toronto Quarterly:* "Anno Domini."

# OTHER BOOKS FROM TUPELO PRESS

*Fasting for Ramadan: Notes from a Spiritual Practice,* Kazim Ali

*This Lamentable City,* Polina Barskova,
edited and introduced by Ilya Kaminsky

*Circle's Apprentice,* Dan Beachy-Quick

*The Vital System,* CM Burroughs

*Stone Lyre: Poems of René Char,*
translated by Nancy Naomi Carlson

*Atlas Hour,* Carol Ann Davis

*New Cathay: Contemporary Chinese Poetry, 1991–2012*
edited by Ming Di

*Sanderlings,* Geri Doran

*The Flight Cage,* Rebecca Dunham

*The Posthumous Affair* (novel), James Friel

*Other Fugitives & Other Strangers,* Rigoberto González

*The Us,* Joan Houlihan

*Nothing Can Make Me Do This* (novel), David Huddle

*Meridian,* Kathleen Jesme

*A God in the House: Poets Talk About Faith,*
edited by Ilya Kaminsky and Katherine Towler

*Manoleria,* Daniel Khalastchi

*Phyla of Joy,* Karen An-hwei Lee

*Lucky Fish,* Aimee Nezhukumatathil

*Long Division,* Alan Michael Parker

*Intimate: An American Family Photo Album,* Paisley Rekdal

*Calendar of Fire,* Lee Sharkey

*The Beginning of the Fields,* Angela Shaw

*Cream of Kohlrabi: Stories,* Floyd Skloot

*The Forest of Sure Things,* Megan Snyder-Camp

*Babel's Moon,* Brandon Som

*Butch Geography,* Stacey Waite

*Dogged Hearts,* Ellen Doré Watson

See our complete backlist at www.tupelopress.org